A TRAVELER IS
QUARANTINED

Lewis Codington

TEN REASONS TO READ IT STRAIGHT THROUGH

In August, it was time for my wife and me to return to Korea, where we have been volunteer teaching English at three schools for North Korean defectors. We had lost the spring term to the Covid pandemic, but we decided to return for the fall term, come what may.

When we arrived at Immigration in Seoul, we were keeping our fingers crossed, hoping that we would be allowed to spend our two week quarantine lockdown at the apartment we had lived in before. With the global spread of the Corona Virus, many countries had instituted a mandatory 14 day isolation for travelers arriving internationally. Following our 15 hour flight from Atlanta, we spent a grueling and exhausting four hour process before being allowed into the country. But our journey was not over. The Customs officials were adamant: without family or property ownership in Korea, all arriving passengers must spend the 14 day lockdown in a government quarantine facility. Realizing that this might be our fate, we had loaded ourselves down with books to read while we passed the days on our own.

But an interesting thing happened to us. Just as we were leaving the United States, I was reminded that one of our North Korean students, during three weeks of hiding in China before he was able to escape to South Korea, had read through a Bible given to him five times in those three weeks. I was really challenged by his example. Could we read through the Bible once...in two weeks? Although it is our regular habit to read the Bible through each year, we had never done so in something close to "one sitting". We were both intrigued and captivated by the idea. Usually when I travel, I will carry a New Testament or small Bible with me to read. But as we became more enthusiastic about this opportunity and challenge, we both packed full Bibles to carry with us. Elsbeth had a small, easy to carry, pocket Bible. But I brought along a 2600 page Study Bible. I divided that number by 14 days and realized that I would need to read close to 200 pages a day (while in Elsbeth's case, about 100 pages a day) in order to complete the challenge. Could we do it? We weren't sure, but we were certainly excited with the idea. I divided up the books of the Bible into 12 days (leaving us a little buffer at the end in case we got bogged down), and we started on page one during our first day of quarantine.

The first two days were the toughest. We had jet lag to contend with, and the Pentateuch (Genesis and Exodus on day one; Leviticus, Numbers, and Deuteronomy on day two) is not exactly light reading to wade through. But we pushed through those days, reading about 7-8 hours a day, pausing to eat and exercise at various intervals. Then followed Israel's history, the books of instruction, the prophets, and finally into the New Testament. On day 12, we arrived at the last book, Revelation, and when we completed the final page, we looked up at each other and smiled. We held up our Bibles, took a selfie, hugged, and then thanked God for the exhilarating privilege we had just experienced. We may never again have a window of opportunity like this with such extended periods of uninterrupted time that allow us to do this. But we both found it to be a wonderful adventure. Here's why:

1) Getting the grand sweep of the Bible reminds us of the BLESSING that is ours in having the whole Bible, which most people down through history have not had.

2) Reading it so quickly shows us more clearly how it all fits together as one overall, UNIFIED MESSAGE in a way that reading it a little at a time does not so easily do.

3) Reading the Old and New Testaments together reveals how the New Testament FULFILLS what the Old Testament pointed to.

4) The CHARACTERS in the Bible become more understandable as their names and stories appear at different points all through the book.

5) We see more clearly who GOD is. His relentless love for everyone, his holiness, and his sovereignty shine through.

6) We see people constantly and repeatedly TURNING AWAY from God. That makes his provision, rescue, and salvation all the more remarkable. God loves us more deeply and

permanently than we will ever be able to fully understand.

7) We see how God uses the MISFITS of the world to carry out his plans. His plans are perfect and infinitely important - they involve people's eternal destinies. And yet, God is pleased to allow us weak people to participate in carrying them out.

8)The breadth and depth of the Bible - it's grand scope - which was written over thousands of years, by dozens of people, all holds together with one theme that is as RELEVANT today as it was when it was written.

9) We see more clearly the devastation caused by SIN - our disobedience to God - down through the ages, and right up to the present day.

10) The Bible is a "MAGICAL" book, in every good sense of that word. It is the one gift God has given us to show us who he is, who we are, what our purpose is on earth, and how we should live. It is the grandest, most spectacular book ever written, and you see that more emphatically when you fly through it quickly.

So, read it! Read through it! Carve out ten days or two weeks to push through it. You will be richer, more grateful, and more in awe for it.

God bless you.

Lewis Codington

August 22 - September 2, 2020

I WONDER...

...if Paul at times may have enjoyed being in prison... "What?? Are you crazy?" Perhaps that's a normal response to a dumb question like that. But, think about it. When he was in prison, Paul didn't have to sew any tents, didn't have to travel or get shipwrecked, didn't have to worry about his next meal, and could read and write uninterrupted, all day long, if he wanted to. Sounds like a pretty good deal to me! When we landed in Seoul last August, we knew we would likely be in for a two week quarantine in a government facility. We were hoping the Immigration folks might have mercy on us and allow us to quarantine in our own apartment, but, though they were all smiles and politeness, they were also firm. "No dice. Nada. Ain't gonna happen on our watch, amigos." But, what we began, with a good measure of fear and trepidation, turned out to be a spiritual highlight that we will never forget...being able to read the whole Bible through in two weeks. It's a little embarrassing to admit that God had to jail me in order to get me to do this...but, still, it was a wonderful experience, and it makes me wonder about Paul's sojourns in prison. (Granted, he probably didn't have clean sheets, AC, delicious Korean food, or a beautiful bay view like we did...) We are about to head back to Korea again, and once more we're hoping to quarantine at home. But, we're preparing for the alternative jail sentence, as well, which means not seeing anyone, and not being able to leave our room the whole time. Actually, this time around, I'm excited about the prospect. I want to do something different from reading all the way through the Bible. I love the Psalms, which teach us so much about God and our relationship with him, and so, I'm planning to read all the way through them, every day, for ten days. I'm preparing myself already. I've picked out ten different versions of the Psalms to take with me...mostly pocket sized, so they won't be too much of a burden to carry. The ones I've selected are:

Christian Standard Bible,
Contemporary English Version,
English Standard Version,
Good News Bible,
King James Version,
Message Bible,
New International Version,
New Living Translation,
New Revised Standard Version, and
Schottenstein Tehillim Interlinear Translation.

I'm excited to see what God may have in store for me as I delve deeply into his Word once again. Digging through all my Bibles makes me realize how terribly rich we are in the current generation to have so many good choices of God's Word. From the list above, only one or two were even available when I was a boy. So, what will we do with all this richness we have in our hands? God wants us to use it for good, for worshipping and honoring him, for reaching out to others.

Jesus, in Matthew 23, was talking to a group of folks just like us...folks who, in their day, had been entrusted with much in the way of spiritual things. And he wasn't happy with what he saw. They had used their privilege and blessing to look down on others, to load people up with burdens, to set themselves in high places for their own benefit. Jesus was angry at them for not using well the blessings God had given them to pass on to others. It's a serious reminder to us: God hasn't blessed us for our own fatness or pleasure...but so that we will use all in our hands to bless others and honor God. That is what he desires, that is what he will check for, one of these days, when we encounter him face to face.

DURING OUR SECOND QUARANTINE...

...in Korea, we are grateful that we were allowed to spend the two weeks locked down at home. When we did this the first time, last August, we spent the days in a government facility (which was actually better than it sounds). We spent that quarantine reading all the way through the Bible, which was a wonderful experience.

This time, I wanted to do something similar, so I brought along with me 12 versions of the Psalms, and I hope to read through a different one each day.

Today, it ended out taking 13 hours (6:15 a.m. to 7:15 p.m.), mainly because I wrote down 30 pages of verses (which I hope to use for a project later) as I was reading. Whew! A long day, but well worth it.

My takeaway from this day spent in the Psalms was four words which summarize what I read again and again. They are:

*Watch

*Word

*Welcome

*Worship

Over and over again, as we travel through this wonderful book of conversations, back and forth between the writer (very often King David) and God, we are struck by how God is watching out for his people.

God's words or commandments (the Bible) are

<u>highlighted as being essential</u> to our health and well-being in life.

<u>God regularly invites and welcomes us into his presence</u>.

And, as we enter God's presence, <u>we should come with an attitude of worship</u>.

It was a great, and rather tiring, day. Try it sometime when you have a day you can block out. Getting the big picture presents us with ideas and impressions that are a little different from reading through the Psalms, one at a time. Enjoy the ride!

TEN REASONS TO READ THE PSALMS STRAIGHT THROUGH...

On day 2 of our quarantine in Korea, I read through the Psalms in 11 hours. When I came to the end of the book, I was overwhelmed with God's greatness and goodness, his love for his imperfect people. I could only get down on the floor and thank our majestic Sovereign of the universe.

As I was reading, 10 things in particular jumped out at me. Here they are, described in 10 words that begin with "I":

1) Invitation - As we read the Psalms, we can hear God inviting us to approach him, to come into his presence. This Almighty God delights in being with us.

2) Infinity - Who is it that invites us into his presence? The One who is infinite in every aspect of his character...his power, existence, understanding, presence, love, righteousness, holiness. This is the God who loves us, the One we meet in the Psalms.

3) Imperfection - At the same time as we see God's greatness, we also see that life is imperfect. The world is a mess, people are a mess, and the writer, time and again, runs to God with all his troubles, because he knows that God is the only One who can deal with his problems.

4) Imminence - This great God of ours is so close and accessible, that we can reach out to him anytime. Whenever we come to him, he hears and listens, he

is always with us. Very often, the writer speaks to God as if they are sitting or walking side by side.

5) Intentionality - As if we are hard of hearing (We are!), we are repeatedly told to seek God...and to obey his commandments. This is not a casual suggestion, not something that just happens. We have to be deliberate in seeking God out. Most all the problems we see around us are due to people not seeking God, and disobeying what he tells us to do.

6) Inoculator - God is the great inoculator. That's not a word we normally associate with God, but we should. Like a physician applying a vaccination against our disease, God provides the inoculation against our selfish sin problem. Repeatedly, God tells us to come to him, so that he can fix us, heal us, save us. He has the solution to what ails us.

7) Intimate - What is so amazing about the Psalms is how it describes God's complete understanding of everything about us...every bone in our body, exactly how many days we are destined to live, all our thoughts. That would be a pretty scary thought if it weren't for the fact that he also loves us so much that we can't even begin to measure his love for us.

8) Instructs - Time and time and time again, the Psalms tell us that God's book, the Bible, teaches us about life, its purpose, how to navigate it, and how to live wisely on this earth.

9) Irrevocable - The Psalms refer frequently to God coming to our rescue, coming to save us, providing our Savior from sin. And, of course, it points to Christ's provision of salvation for us, a salvation that

is permanent, that can't be changed, and can't be taken away from us.

10) Individual - Much of the Old Testament, and even the New Testament, addresses God's people in how they are to live together. The Psalms are very individualistic. They are addressed to you, to me. The promises, God's rescue, his presence...all these things are spoken directly to you and to me. The book carries a message that is specifically tailored to you.

What an amazing and great book! I was stunned by its magnificent message for us right now. Jump into it today!

DURING OUR QUARANTINE DAY 3,

I read through a Jewish translation of the Psalms. It contains the Hebrew, along with the English translation of the Hebrew words. It was tricky to read the English, as it followed the Hebrew, which is laid out on the page, from right to left (instead of left to right across the page as we are used to in English!). I was struck by how closely the English words in this Jewish Bible match our Christian translations, so it gives me confidence that our versions have been very well translated from the original Hebrew.

Two main thoughts impressed me today as I read:

1) God is very, very close to us. He is like a friend sitting with us in our living room...near us, accessible to us, listening to us, in easy conversation with us.

2) God is infinite. His power, understanding, knowledge, and greatness are overpowering to us. We can't really comprehend how great he is. And yet, amazingly, he wants to be with us. We are the ones he wants to spend time with and get to know. What a magnificent God we have!

Read all about him in the Psalms!

FIFTY "P'S" FROM THE POD OF PSALMS

Here's something fun (and very rewarding) if you have a fair chunk of free time this weekend. **On our fourth day of quarantine** in Seoul, as I was again reading through the Psalms, I tried to come up with as many meaningful words from the text that start with the letter "p". (If you want to try it, you could just as easily try words starting with c, r, s, or some other letter.)

So, here are the nearly 50 "p's" in the pod of Psalms that jumped out at me:

* practical - God's Word relates to our everyday life.

* protective - God is very attentive to us.

* personal - God is right here with us; he's not far off.

* pleasant - God treats us this way, not like some cold, distant person.

* permanent - God focuses on eternal, enduring things.

* perplexing - If there is one thing we see loudly in the Psalms, it is that his people didn't understand God and how he works.

* pure - There is nothing bad or evil in God.

* perfect - This word explains much about God.

* promises - The Psalms are filled with wonderful statements that God makes to us...and carries through.

* preserves - God cares for, keeps, and watches over us.

* portion - The Psalms sometimes talk about God being "our portion"...he's what we need, he's all that we need.

* praise - If you're not sure what to do, try this toward God. You won't go wrong!

* place - God has, God is, a special place for us.

* people - These are the creations that God cares most for and is most attentive to.

* proclaim - The universe speaks to us of God's existence, greatness, and goodness. And we are also supposed to do the same about him to others.

* precepts - God's Word that he has given to us is perfect and what we need in this life.

* purpose - God directs and has clear plans for what he is unfolding in the world.

* prosper - God plans this for us, in a way that is congruent with his character, not necessarily with ours!

* path - The journey that God has us on is the one that is right for us.

* pursue - God chases after us because he loves us.

* propitiation - God's salvation for us is adequate, it's what we need, it covers our sinfulness.

* provide - God gives us, not what we want, but what we need.

* present - God is right here with us.

* patient - God is unendingly patient with us. When we don't understand him, we also need to be patient and trust him.

* plead - God wants us to take him seriously, to come to him earnestly, to open our hearts pleadingly to

him.

* possession - We belong to God; that's our safest place to be.

* power - God's speech through events in the world, his control over the universe, demonstrate his power.

* peace - This is what God desires for us...a relationship that is at peace with him.

* potentate - If there is one Sovereign, Almighty Being in the universe, which there is, it is God.

* passing - Life is certainly passing; God's anger is also passing and is often swallowed up by his love for us.

* pride - My biggest problem.

* public - Where God wants us to live; where he wants us to praise him.

* pain - In case we weren't sure of it before, the Psalms let's us know pretty emphatically that this life has plenty of it.

* plunders - You ready for this? God plunders our sin with his unending grace and love.

* please - Our job in this world is very simple: please God.

* pour - God dumps his love on us. In turn, he wants us to unload our hearts on him.

* perspective - I tend to focus on what I like, what is important to me, what makes me feel good. God is less complicated than that. He focuses on eternal things.

* particular - What God provides for us...our salvation...is tailor made to meet our need.

* plants - Isn't it wonderful! God provides a seemingly infinite array of beautiful, fascinating, satisfying plants for our pleasure, study, food, clothing, shelter...

* parent - God loves us like the most tender parent. That's what he wants to be to us.

* pilgrimage - If the shoe sometimes feels like it doesn't fit in life...it's because it doesn't. We don't belong here. This is not our home. We're just passing through briefly.

* perform - You like wonderful performances? God executed the most dazzling performance when he created all the wonders of this universe.

* prayer - Pray. Just pray. Talk to God. Bring your heart, your needs, your desires to him.

* pasture - One of the most beautiful pictures is to drive by a sprawling field, full of contentedly grazing animals. That's what God has in mind for us as we rest in him.

* practice - We can't exactly walk through this life with God if we don't carry out and put into motion what he tells us to do.

* prisoners - We may not always understand it fully, but we are slaves to the selfish sin that is in us. God wants to set us free from those shackles, so that we are no longer prisoners of evil.

* prostitute - This is not a pleasant word in any of our minds. But God tells us that when we disobey him, we become prostitutes to sin and the devil...in other words, it's serious.

* pity - In every good sense of the word, God cares for

us with the greatest of care and concern.

* pleasure - When we follow God, he loads us down with wonderful things. (But, remember, these are not the same kinds of pleasures that Santa brings us.)

Now...I can't wait for you to share with us all the words you find in the Psalms, starting with some particular letter!

FIFTY "S" WORDS FROM THE PSALMS

Yesterday I enjoyed thinking about words suggested in the Psalms beginning with the letter "P". So, **today, I thought I would try focusing on words beginning with the letter "S"**...and when the dust settled, I had found almost exactly as many as I found yesterday. Here they are:

* sacred - God is holy and righteousness.

* sacrifice - What we bring to God is a reflection of what is inside of us. When we bring our thanks, even in pain, God receives them as an offering to him.

* safety - When we are in God's care, we are in this place.

* satisfy - A lot of people and things can being us enjoyment. There is only one Person who can give us this.

* save - A relationship with God, walking with him, protects us from a multitude of sin and heartache.

* say - When God tells us something, we better listen.

* scatters - God seems to be pretty careless in the way he spreads his blessings around.

* secure - In God's care, our future can be described in this way.

* see - If we will look around us, much to thank God for will be in evidence all around us.

* seek - We need to be deliberate and intentional about following after God.

* send - God is deliberate in dispatching goodness to

us.

* sensitive - God cares about us and is aware of our needs.

* servant - It is wise for us to remember our position before God, including this aspect.

* shadow - God covers us like a refreshing tree in the summertime.

* shelter - Although life seems to be full of dangers, there are many that God protects us from, even when we are unaware of it.

* shepherd - God looks after us as the tenderest of care givers.

* shield - God protects us from many things.

* shines - God's greatness is bright all across the universe.

* should - When God tells us something in his Word, it's more than just a suggestion.

* shows - God delights to teach us many things.

* side - God stays right close to us, as if we are walking next to each other.

* sight - When we follow God, our ability to see what is really important sharpens.

* silent - Although God loves us to bare our soul to him, it is also very appropriate for us to spend time quietly before him, reflecting on whose presence we are in.

* sin - This is an infection that is always with us. But God isn't afraid of it and will help us deal with it if we allow him to.

* sing - God delights for us to come to him this way, good tune or no.

* sleep- This can be peaceful when we lay all our cares at God's feet. But sometimes, God will disrupt this because he really wants to spend time with us.

* slow - When I don't get my way, I can be very quick to react in anger. But God doesn't enjoy getting angry at us, so he usually responds in this way to our disobedience.

* so - God's laws are there for a reason, for our good....so...we would do well, and save ourselves and those around us a lot of discomfort by following them.

* son - Gods looks at us as if we are his favorite child.

* sorrow - This life does seem to have plenty of these, so we shouldn't be overly surprised by their appearance at our door.

* sounds - God loves for us to make these in a joyful way!

* sovereign - There is no one and no thing higher than God.

* speaks - God communicates to us...through his Word, his creation, our experiences...

* spreads - God loves to pour out his goodness on us.

* steady - God's love for us is like this, as the day is long.

* still - However many times I blow it, God keeps coming after me with his love.

* stop - God's goodness and love can't be interfered with.

* straight - The path of following God can be described in this way.

* stranger - God especially loves these kinds of

people.

* stream - Rushing water always conveys life and health and blessing. That's how God is toward us.

* strength - God's power can knock over mountains and jolt oceans. Thankfully, he's a good God.

* stronghold - God is a safe place for us to run to with our needs.

* study - God has given us time, days, years, so that we can learn about him.

* subdues - God can and does stop evil in its tracks...in ways we are unaware of or can't yet see.

* succeed - At the end of the day, when we follow God, he tells us we won't fail.

* sunrise - The beginning of a new day conveys the idea of hope and a fresh start...the same thing that God gives us repeatedly.

* supplies - When we have spiritual needs, this is what God does for us.

* support - God provides for us.

* supreme - God is the final, ultimate, only, authority we need to be concerned about.

* surrounds - God loves to overdose us in compassion and goodness.

* swift - Although we miss it often, or frequently misunderstand it, God is already sending responses to our needs even as we are verbalizing them.

I love the Psalms! Don't we have a great God!

77 REASONS WHY GOD ALLOWS SUFFERING... (FROM THE PSALMS)

How many people miss 2020 already? Huh, I can't hear you? Anyone? Probably not. I've heard more that a few people say, "Good riddance! May it never happen again!" I have been praying during the year that it would turn people's attention to God. Still, we do wonder why God allowed us to go through it. At the risk of having missed some, listed below are about 77 suggestions of why God permits us to go through suffering, misery, affliction...whatever you want to call it...gleaned from my **reading once more through the Psalms today**, along with the chapters and verses that reflect these ideas.

It is also very good to remind ourselves, as we ponder these things, that God's love for us is as high as the heavens (103:11), that his love never fails (136:1), that he is completely kind (145:17), and that he is too wonderful to even be described (150:2)...so, clearly there is an element of mystery involved in how and why God uses suffering.

With that in mind, here we go:

* 3:5-6   We learn from our suffering.
* 11:5   God tests us through it.
* 13:5   We learn to be thankful.
* 16:7   It reminds us of God.
* 17:14   It presents an opportunity for God to

provide for us.

* 18:3,16   God saves us in our sufferings.

* 20:1   It turns our attention to God.

* 22:6,15   It shows us who we are...in need of God.

* 22:27   It grabs people's attention. (Is he talking about Covid here?)

* 23:4   We learn that God's presence is sufficient.

* 25:16   C.S. Lewis famously said that: "We read to know we are not alone."

         Apparently, God also uses suffering to remind us that we're not alone.

* 25:18   We learn of our sinfulness.

* 26:2   It reveals who we are.

* 27:1   It dispels our fears.

* 27:11   It teaches us to follow God.

* 28:1   It teaches us to trust in God.

* 29:3   It helps us see and hear God.

* 30:5   It teaches us the greatness of God's mercy.

* 31:7   God shows us his care for us.

* 31:19   People have an opportunity to see who God is.

* 31:22   It teaches us to seek God.

* 32:2   God forgives us when we are reminded to acknowledge our sins.

* 33:10   God reveals his good plans in the midst of hardship.

* 33:20   God protects us.

* 34:4   It turns our attention to God and away from our circumstances.

* 34:5   It gives us the possibility of succeeding by turning our focus to God.

* 34:7   It provides the opportunity for God's angels to protect us.

* 34:10   We will be blessed with what is good.

* 34:17   It teaches us to pray.

* 34:19   God will carry us through.

* 34:22   It can save us from punishment.

* 35:18   It gives an opportunity to bless other believers.

* 37:7   We learn to be patient in tribulation.

* 37:24   It gives us the opportunity to experience God's presence.

* 37:33   We learn whether we're on God's side.

* 38:5   It reveals our sinfulness.

* 39:11   We are being punished for our disobedience.

* 40:3   It can be a witness to many people.

* 40:6   It teaches us to listen and obey.

* 42:5   It teaches us to trust in God.

* 44:23   It teaches us to persevere in seeking God.

* 46:10   It teaches us who God is.

* 47:3   God brings justice to a broken world.

* 48:3   It is a consequence of people's sinfulness.

* 48:13-14 To help us know what to tell others about God.

* 49:17   It teaches us not to trust in wealth.

* 50:9   It reveals the artificial trappings of religion.

* 50:15   It teaches us to honor God.

* 50:22   To wake us up!

* 60:3-4   To alert us to danger.

* 62:3,5   To teach us to have peace with God.

* 63:3   To teach us God's love.

* 64:7-8 To demonstrate God's awesome power.
* 66:10,12 To bring us to a better place.
* 73:23,26 To teach us a proper perspective.
* 77:2,11 To remind us of God's goodness.
* 78:34   To teach us to turn away from sin.
* 81:6-7   Because sometimes we don't listen.
* 88:18   At our lowest, hard times remind us that we can still unburden ourselves
           to God.
* 90:10,14 Teaches us that God's love satisfies.
* 91:14-16 We see God's provision and care in the long run.
* 97:10-11 To give us guidance and peace.
* 105:17-19 Sometimes, as in the case of Joseph, our sufferings are part of a bigger
           rescue plan.
* 105:42 To give God the opportunity to keep his promises.
* 109:26-27 To demonstrate to others God's salvation.
* 119:25 To turn our attention back to God's Word.
* 119:39 To protect us, through God's Word.
* 119:50 To provide comfort through God's Word.
* 126:6   To provide celebration for a spiritual harvest.
* 127:4   There is blessing in a lot of kids...whether they are a source of tribulation is
           another question...
* 130:1,3 It reminds us of God's forgiveness.
* 135:9 It can be used to punish evil.
* 140:11-12 To demonstrate God's justice.

* 142:7 To teach me to praise God.
* 143:7-8 To learn even more about how much God loves us.
* 145:15 To show us how God provides.
* 146:7 To show God's merciful kindness.

(On a personal note, being locked up for two weeks of quarantine upon entering Korea, not able to go out even once, can seem like a kind of suffering. Certainly not something I would have chosen or asked for. But this enforced short leash, which involves checking in with the authorities twice a day, has provided the opportunity for me to read several times through the Psalms, something under normal conditions, I'm sure I wouldn't get around to doing. So, what has been, on the one hand, a major hassle or inconvenience, God has used to bless me greatly. And that's exactly what we see about suffering in the Psalms...there is very often a good aspect to our suffering that most probably is the reason God brings these things into our lives.)

IN THE LAST NINE DAYS,

I've greatly enjoyed reading through the Psalms each day while in quarantine (i.e. can't leave our apartment), a different version each day: Amplified Bible, New Living Translation, New Catholic Version, New Revised Standard, Christian Standard, Schottenstein Jewish Edition, English Standard, Good News, and today the King James Version.

The KJV has some beautiful phrases, such as in 145:8..."The Lord is gracious, and full of compassion, slow to anger, and of great mercy."

It also contains a few quaint words that leave you scratching your head, such as: satest, privily, inditing (hint: not a legal term), holpen, minished, usest, gins (hint: not a drink), garner, unicorn (no idea!)

I wrote down one word to summarize each of the 150 chapters:

Answer 3

Awe 2

Blessing

Call 2

Clarity

Confess

Creation 2

Cry

Desire

Dominion

Dwelling

End
Enemies
Evil
Faithful
Family
Fellowship
Focus
Follow
Fools
Forgiveness 2
Gracious
Great 3
Guide
Hardship
Hear 2
Heaven
Help 12
Heritage
Honor
Hurry
Judge 2
Justice 8
Keeps
King 2
Lament
Leads
Listen
Longing 2
Love
Mercy 4
Mighty 2

Opposition
Path
Persecution
Ponder
Power 3
Praise 11
Pray
Presence
Protection
Recount
Reflect 2
Refuge
Reigns
Rejoice
Remember 2
Repent
Rescue 2
Restore 2
Righteous
Ruler 3
Save 4
Security 2
Servant
Shelter
Sing 2
Sovereign 2
Tell
Thanks 6
Trust 2
Wait 2
Watch

Wicked 3
With
Words 2
Worship 5
Zion
A quick glance over these words reveals to us a God who welcomes and invites us to come to him for help, he wants to make things right, and that we should praise and thank and worship him. Fairly straightforward, really.

SEVENTY-FIVE PS"A"LMS WORDS IN PSALMS

From my reading of the Psalms today:

* abandon - If we belong to God, he will never leave us.

* abhors - God really does not like evil.

* abide - Our task in life is to walk with, to live with, God.

* able - God equips us to live for him.

* abominable - I hate to think of what my disobedience looks like to God.

* abounding - There's really not enough room in the world for God's love for us.

* about - God is all around us, keeping watch over us.

* above - God is in heaven, watching out for us.

* Abraham - The attention given to this man is a picture of the attention God pours out on us as well.

* abroad - Tell about God's love to everyone, everywhere.

* abundance - God's grace toward us will never run out.

* accepts - When we come to God in prayer, he hears and receives us.

* accomplish - God's salvation on our behalf is a done deal, completed.

* according - When God acts in the universe, he does so in line with his good and loving character.

* account - Everything we have is entrusted to us...on loan, if you will...and we will one day be

required to give a reporting of what we did with everything God has placed in our hands.

* accuse - What the devil tries to do to us...but God covers us if we are trusting in him.

* acknowledge - There aren't many of us who would imagine that we are not selfish. God expects us to confess and turn from our selfish disobedience.

* acquaint - This is what we're supposed to spend the rest of our lives doing with God.

* adder - This is just a fancy word for that nasty, slithering reptile. They can't touch us without God's permission.

* adoration - Our thoughts toward God should be along this line.

* adversity- There is plenty in the Psalms that talks about the struggles and disappointments in life. They are real; they will come knocking.

* afar - Sometimes God can seem very distant from us. Don't believe your feelings.

* afflicted - When we are hurting, God hears us and sees us.

* after - We should pursue, seek God.

* again - God keeps forgiving us.

* against - When we reject God, he is opposed to us.

* aha - God is scornful of the devil's attempts to trip him up.

* ails - God heals our spiritual diseases.

* aim - God's attention is focused on us.

* alarm - When we are in a desperate situation, we get God's attention.

* all - Everyone who seeks God is blessed.

* allied - When we give our lives to God, we're on the same team, the one that will come out on top.

* alone - Ultimately, God is the only one who can truly help our heart problem.

* aloud - God loves us to worship him together, noisily.

* altar - Our prayers are so important and special to God that he receives them as an important sacrifice.

* always - God never forgets us.

* ambush - What evil tries to do to us. Be alert.

* among - God looks for pleasing attitudes and obedience within us.

* ancient - God has been around a long time...before time began.

* and - We never come to the end of God's grace...there is always more to come.

* angels - God has special agents whose job is to watch out for us.

* anger - Our disobedience creates this response in God.

* announce - Let's tell the world about this wonderful God.

* anoints - As he did to his followers in the Old Testament, God appoints a special task for us to do on his behalf.

* another - When we turn away from or disobey God, we are, in effect, chasing a different god.

* answers - Parents can be so exasperating in their responses to their children's requests. God does respond to our requests...but, we can get pretty exasperated with his responses as well.

* anxious - When I fret and bring my concerns to him, God comes to my rescue.

* any - Sometimes God looks over the world and wonders if there is even one good person down here.

* apart - God wants us to set our life aside especially to honor him.

* appeal - Bring our requests to God.

* appears - God enters our life in a variety of ways.

* apple - In God's eyes, we are his very own, special, choice fruit that he has his eye on.

* appoints - God directs and controls what happens in the world.

* arises - When we call to God, we get his attention...and he gets up in response to us.

* arms - God's encircle us with these.

* army - God has a vast array of followers serving him.

* around - God encircles us as a mother does to her newborn baby.

* arrogance - Our biggest problem.

* arrows - God uses his best weapons against evil.

* ascend - Let's send our prayers up God's way.

* ascribe - We should give honor and glory to God.

* ashamed - When we bring our guilt to God, he covers us and heals us.

* aside - We need to stay alert so that we aren't turned away from God.

* ask - God invites us to.

* assails - Evil is always trying to come against us.

* assembly - There is a huge mass of people who God has saved and gathered. We will get to meet them all

in heaven one day.

* astounds - Our response to God's power.

* at - God's attention is directed toward us.

* atone - God provides for our needs to restore our relationship with him.

* attention - Something God gives us a lot of.

* avenger - This is a real word in God's world. It's what he does against evil.

* avoid - Stay away from evil.

* awake - It's wonderful to know that when the new day dawns, God is still with us.

* away - God will send the wicked packing one day.

* awe - Our attitude toward God.

* awesome - The God we have.

***50 PSA"L"MS WORDS
IN THE PSALMS***

In my reading through the Psalms today, I came up with these words beginning with "L":

* labor - What we should do for God.

* lack - With God, we're not short of anything.

* lamb - God treats and looks upon us as his favorite.

* lament - How we should feel about our sin.

* lamp - God guides our way.

* land - In a spiritual sense, God has a great expanse for us.

* languish - How we are spiritually without God.

* large - God has big plans and a big place for us.

* last - In God's economy, we are never here.

* laud - Our attitude to God.

* laugh - God responds in humor to people's efforts to thwart him.

* law - God's ways and precepts are perfect.

* lay - God says we can rest in his presence.

* lead - God shows us the way.

* lean - God loves for us to rest on him.

* leanness - What happens when we are far from God.

* leap - God can do great things in our lives, even helping us jump over a wall if need be.

* leave - Not something God will do to us.

* lend - Something God does generously for us.

* leniency- God's attitude to us.

* lest - God does what he can for us so that we can

stay close to him.

* level - God's path.

* leviathan - I'm not quite sure what this is...but it is a reminder of God's greatness, if nothing else!

* liberty - What we have in God.

* lice - These little bitty critters are a reminder that sometimes God may send something our way to get our attention.

* lies - Not something we want to try with God.

* life - What God gives us.

* lifeless- Things we put our confidence in apart from God.

* lift - What God does for us.

* light - What God truly is.

* lightning - Similar to when God speaks.

* like - God's Word is full of examples for us.

* limits - The bad things in this life are not permanent.

* lion - God is the king and sometimes roars loudly.

* lips - For the purpose of praising God.

* listen - To God...he also hears us.

* little - Our time here is brief.

* live - Our true existence is with God.

* loathe - What God (and hopefully we) thinks of our selfishness.

* lofty - God is beyond us.

* lonely - Sometimes we will have this experience because life is not how God originally planned or intended it to be.

* long - How we should feel toward God.

* looks - God watches over us and the whole earth.

* Lord - One of the best descriptive words for God.

* lose - The things that we value and give up for God are small compared to what we gain.

* loud - Sometimes God is quiet, other times he really needs to get our attention.

* love - As if this word isn't quite sufficient, the Psalms frequently talk about God's lovingkindness for us.

* low - The people we would consider not important, are not so to God.

* loyal - A word that describes God.

* lust - Watch out!

* luxuriant - Places where God wants us to rest.

* lyre - I'm not sure that this is either, but it's a reminder that worship to God can take many forms and make many noises.

A wonderful exercise!

WHO IS GOD?

What is he like? The Psalms tell us a lot about his attributes and behavior. In a nutshell, the book tells us that God is great (147:5), good (145:9) and gracious (103:4). **As I read through the Psalms today**, I jotted down nearly 200 aspects of this God we worship. Here they are, with a reference that conveys each thought.

He/his:

* Accepts our prayers. 5:2
* Is accessible. 27:8
* Acts are undergirded with love. 136:4
* Acts to save us. 12:5
* Is all that is important. 16:5
* Is Almighty. 22:28
* Is angry at his enemies. 2:5
* Is angry for our distress. 18:7
* Answers us. 3:4
* Arms us. 18:39
* Attacks his enemies. 3:7
* Is beautiful. 27:4
* Is beyond description. 40:5
* Blesses us. 2:12
* Brightness is seen in nature. 18:12
* Is brilliant in his brightness. 4:6
* Brings down evil. 17:13
* Broadens our path. 18:36
* Carries our burdens. 68:19
* Chooses to love us. 47:4

* Chooses world leaders. 2:6
* Is celebrated by nature. 98:7
* Is to be celebrated. 2:11
* Commands us. 17:4
* Confides in us. 25:14
* Considers our pain. 10:14
* Considers us righteous when we are covered by Christ's sacrifice. 18:20
* Controls nations. 43:2
* Controls nature. 18:9
* Counsels us. 16:7
* Covers us. 5:17
* Created us great. 8:5
* Creates wisely. 104:24
* Is the Creator. 8:3
* Crushes us. 44:39
* Defends the needy. 10:18
* Delights in us. 18:19
* Delivers us. 3:7
* Is deserving of awe. 2:11
* Is deserving of our offerings. 4:5
* Desires to engage us. 119:12
* Directs human affairs. 105:15
* Displays his glory. 8:1
* Displays his wrath. 7:11
* Doesn't ignore us. 9:12
* Doesn't scorn us. 22:24
* Encamps around us. 34:7
* Encourages us. 10:17
* Has entrusted much into our hands. 8:6
* Is eternal. 102:25

* Is the eternal King and Ruler. 10:16
* Is the Everlasting God. 48:14
* Examines us. 11:4
* Expands our lives. 18:19
* Expands our path. 18:36
* Expresses himself in nature. 18:13
* Is faithful. 18:25
* Faithfulness is unmeasurable. 36:5
* Is a Father to us. 2:7
* Favors us. 5:12
* Favors us forever. 30:15
* Is fearful. 2:11
* Fills us with good. 81:10
* Forgives us. 32:1
* Is a fortress for us. 18:2
* Frees us. 25:15
* Gives us a good future forever. 23:6
* Gives us a good inheritance. 16:6
* Gives us joy forever. 16:11
* Gives us rest. 23:2
* Gives us security. 4:8
* Is glorious! 8:1
* Is the only God. 5:2
* Is good. 13:6
* Is the only good we have. 16:2
* Guards us. 25:20
* Guides and heals us. 23:2-3
* Hands hold us. 31:15
* Has a place for everyone. 84:3
* Hates wickedness. 5:4
* Heals us. 6:2

* Hears us. 4:1
* Helps orphans. 10:14
* Helps us advance. 18:29
* Helps us always. 46:1
* Helps us build our lives. 127:1
* Hides us in his shadow. 17:8
* Helps us stand. 18:33
* Is holy. 3:4
* Is honored by our praise. 8:2
* Humbles his enemies. 18:39
* Instructs us. 16:7
* Invites us to gather with him. 7:7
* Invites us to ask of him. 2:8
* Is the joy giver. 4:7
* Is the Judge. 1:5
* Judges fairly. 9:8
* Keeps us as the apple of his eye. 17:8
* Keeps us going. 18:28
* Is the King. 5:2
* Knows us for our own good. 139:5
* Laughs at his enemies. 2:4
* Uses his law to protect us. 119:156
* Is the law giver. 1:2
* Leads us. 5:8
* Lifts us up. 3:3
* Is light for us. 27:1
* Listens to us. 10:17
* Lives with the righteous. 15:2
* Love is unmeasurable. 36:5
* Loves us greatly. 5:7
* Loves unendingly. 6:4

* Loves unfailingly. 13:5
* Makes himself known. 57:13
* Makes us glad. 92:4
* Makes us great. 18:35
* Makes right things that are wrong. 7:8
* Makes use of nature. 29:10
* Is majestic. 8:1
* Meets all our needs. 34:9
* Is merciful. 4:1
* Never abandons us. 16:10
* Owns everything. 2:8
* Is perfect in word and deed. 18:30
* Permits us to tell others about him. 51:13
* Is persistent in pursuing us. 78:38
* Is pleased by us. 19:14
* Prepares our future 23:5
* Is present within us. 14:5
* Preserves us. 31:23
* Pressures us. 32:4
* Prospers even the wicked. 10:5
* Provides rest for our souls. 62:1
* Punishes us. 39:10
* Reaches down to us. 18:16
* Refreshes us. 23:3
* Reveals himself to us. 18:25
* Rebukes his enemies. 2:5
* Receives honor from us. 50:23
* Redirects us. 6:4
* Is a refuge for us. 2:11
* Is the relief giver. 4:1
* Removes our shame. 34:5

* Requires an accounting of what he's placed in our hands. 10:15
* Rescues us. 17:13
* Responds quickly to evil. 2:12
* Restores us. 14:7
* Rewards us as if we are righteous. 18:20
* Is righteous. 4:1
* Is a Rock for us. 18:2
* Rules on earth. 11:4
* Rules in heaven. 11:4
* Is a safe place for us. 31:5
* Satisfies us. 17:15
* Saves us. 6:4
* Scoffs at his enemies. 2:4
* Sees everyone. 11:4
* Sees our pain and trouble. 10:14
* Sets us apart. 4:3
* Is a shepherd to us. 23:1
* Shields us. 3:3
* Shows his love. 31:21
* Spares and protects us. 30:3
* Spoke creation into existence. 32:6
* Straightens our pathway. 5:8
* Strengthens us with his presence. 16:8
* Is strong. 24:8
* Is our stronghold. 18:2
* Supports us. 18:18
* Surrounds us. 5:12
* Sustains us. 3:5
* Teaches us. 71:17
* Terrifies his enemies. 2:5

* Tests us. 17:3
* Trains us. 18:34
* Is trustworthy. 4:5
* Turns things around. 18:28
* Turns toward us. 17:6
* Understands our pain. 31:7
* Understands people. 94:11
* Values life. 49:7
* Wants to work in our lives. 141:3
* Watches over us. 1:6
* Welcomes us. 5:7
* Will be honored. 46:10
* Will be seen by us. 11:7
* Won't forget the needy. 9:18
* Words are perfect. 17:8
* Words are wise, give joy, give light, reward, give warning. 19:8-11
* Is working. 103:6
* Is worthy of praise. 7:17
* Is worthy to be talked about. 9:1
* Is full of wrath against his enemies. 2:5

AS I WAS DOING MY USUAL...

...**reading through Psalms today**, something happened that I just have to share.

Yes, I know I'm a slow learner, but a little word jumped out at me today that is probably one of the most important words in the Bible...and I'm not sure I especially noticed it before.

(OK, yes, "God" is important, too, however, I'm talking about another little word.)

Really, it's a game changer. It simply changes everything...our whole perspective on life...everything.

So, what is the little word, you may be wondering...

But...

Yes, that's it: but.

As I was reading the 150 chapters today, I wrote down nine pages of "but" verses, and they are amazing...and, really, exactly what we need in today's crazy world.

Why is that word so important?

1) It reminds us that what comes before (usually something bad) is not the end of the story...more is going on than first meets the eye.

2) It reminds us that the first glance circumstances around us are not what is most important. Other dynamics are going on that we need to be aware of.

3) Most important, all these verses remind us of who's in charge, who has the final word, why we don't need to worry...that all will be well in the end...

(provided we have things right with that other little word: God).

In 2 Corinthians, Paul reminds us of exactly the same thing. He tells us that what we see around us is not all that's happening, is not in many cases really even all that important, that there is a much bigger dynamic going on that we can easily forget about. That's a wonderful reminder, especially today.

I don't know about you, but the next time someone asks me what I'm worried about, I'm going to respond, "Well, I would be worried, but..."

Here's what I copied down today:

But unfailing love surrounds those who
trust the Lord.   Psalm 32:10
But the Lord's plans stand firm forever
    Psalm 33:11
But the Lord watches over those who
fear him, those who rely on his
unfailing love.   Psalm 33:18
But the Lord comes to the rescue each
time.   Psalm 34:19
But the Lord will redeem those who
serve him.   Psalm 34:22
But the Lord takes care of the godly.
    Psalm 37:17
But each day the Lord pours his
unfailing love upon me.   Ps. 42:8

But as for me, God will redeem my life.
    Psalm 49:15
But giving thanks is a sacrifice that
truly honors me.   Psalm 50:23
But God is my helper.   Psalm 54:4
But I will call on God, and the Lord
will rescue me.   Psalm 55:16
But when I am afraid, I will put
my trust in you.   Psalm 56:3
But you have raised a banner for
those who fear you — a rallying
point in the face of attack. Ps. 60:4
But you brought us to a place of
great abundance.   Psalm 66:12

But God did listen! He paid attention to my prayer. Psalm 66:19

But let the godly rejoice. Let them be joyful in God's presence. B. 68:3

But I keep praying to you, Lord. B. 69:13

But may all who search for you be filled with joy and gladness in you. Psalm 70:4

But you will restore me to life again. Psalm 71:20

But God remains the strength of my heart. Psalm 73:26

But as for me, how good it is to be near God! Psalm 73:28

But as for me, I will always proclaim what God has done. Psalm 75:9

But then I recall all you have done, O Lord; I remember your wonderful deeds of long ago. Psalm 77:11

But he commanded the skies to open; he opened the doors of heaven. Psalm 78:23

But he led his own people like a flock of sheep, guiding them safely through the wilderness. Psalm 78:52

But you, O Lord, are a God of compassion and mercy, slow to get angry and filled with unfailing love and faithfulness. Psalm 86:15

But your unfailing love, O Lord,
supported me. Psalm 94:18
But the Lord is my fortress; my God
is the mighty rock where I hide.
Psalm 94:22
But the Lord made the heavens! P. 96:5
But you, O Lord, will sit on your throne
forever. Psalm 102:12
But the love of the Lord remains
forever with those who fear him. P.103:17
But he rescues the poor from trouble.
Psalm 107:41
But I will give repeated thanks to
the Lord, praising him to everyone.
Psalm 109:30

But he himself will be refreshed
from brooks along the way. Ps. 110:7
But to your name goes all the glory
for your unfailing love and faithfulness.
Psalm 115:1
But we can praise the Lord both
now and forever. Psalm 115:18
But the Lord rescued me. Psalm 118:13
But I do not turn away from your
instructions. Psalm 119:51
But now I closely follow your Word. Ps.119:67
But in truth I obey your commandments
with all my heart. Psalm 119:69
But I delight in your instructions.
Psalm 119:70

But I have not forgotten to obey your
decrees.   Psalm 119:93
But I refused to abandon your
commandments   Psalm 119:87
But I will not stop obeying your
instructions   Psalm 119:109
But I will not turn from your
commandments.   Psalm 119:110
But I love your instructions. P. 119:113
But I don't forget your commandments.
                 Psalm 119:141
But they sing as they return with
the harvest.   Psalm 126:6
But the Lord is good. Psalm 129:4

But you offer forgiveness   P. 130:4
But even in darkness I cannot hide
from you.   Psalm 139:12
But they delight in the law of the
Lord   Psalm 1:2
But you, O Lord, are a shield
around me.   Psalm 3:3
But let all who take refuge in you
rejoice.   Psalm 5:11
But the needy will not be ignored
forever.   Psalm 9:18
But the Lord will protect his people
                 Psalm 14:6
But in my distress I cried out to the Lord
                 Psalm 18:6

Made in the USA
Columbia, SC
19 August 2024

40210894R00033